DREAMING FOREVER:
LIFEMARE EDITION

DREAMING FOREVER: LIFEMARE EDITION

Poems

Dolapo Demuren

A Better Tomorrow Publishing

A Better Tomorrow Publishing
P.O. Box 2975
Upper Marlboro, MD 20773-2975
301 980-8541

First printing 2010

ISBN: 978-0-9795768-3-6

LCCN: 2010908276

Library of Congress Cataloging in Publication Data is available.

Editing, design and production coordinated by
A Better Tomorrow Publishing; www.abtpub.com

ATTENTION CORPORATIONS, UNIVERSITIES, COLLEGES, HIGH SCHOOLS AND PROFESSIONAL ORGANIZATIONS: Quantity discounts are available on bulk purchases of this book for educational or gift purposes. Special books or book excerpts can also be created to fit specific needs. For information, please contact:

A Better Tomorrow Publishing
P.O. Box 2975
Upper Marlboro, MD 20773-2975
1-866-980-8541
www.abtpub.com

Dedication

This book is dedicated to my mother and father, and also to Mrs. Adoline Shodiya for making all of this possible.

Table of Contents

Unattainable

Sequence 1. Dream

Sequence 2. Nightmares

Sequence 3. Bliss

Sequence 5. Loner

Autumn's Rose

Dreaming Forever: Thoughts

Author's Note

Enjoy.

UNATTAINABLE

Autumn

She wrote our names
on the bark of a redwood tree
the imprints hardened
as the sap poured—
until its motion stilled
at the richness of the soil

She *turned* around
and her soles kissed the faces
of the fallen leaves
as she walked to me

"Victims of Autumn"
is what we called them

We laughed,
I held her
and felt her hair dance
on the edge of my cheeks
and the subtle breeze of the wind
on the tips of my fingers
as I raced my hands
down her back
watching her

brunette beauty
turn to bronze
as the sunlight showered her
with its rays of love

Bringing warmth to her and I
making each spec of light
reveal a story
to unfold her
while creating literature
on her skin

Her chest thumped with mine
her eyes escaped in mine
and mine in hers
I found that there was no time for words
she wanted all of me
and gave me all of her

A beloved memory
a part of my forever

Now as I reminisce—
I see this winter has gotten colder
its silvers and gold are worth much to me now

You are my
youthful *desire*
and sadly—
nothing *more*
And although that day was the first time
I expressed myself through
the unspoken language of my heart

I know
it would have been better
if I loved you—

If I had loved
Autumn

June 9th

Our experiences
will forever be in my heart
but you're just a *part*
of something that I don't
want to find myself lost in

I have come to realize
I wanted a *part* of you
I could never have,
and now it seems
we have to be apart
for me to *feel*
real again

I know soon another man
will have you
and what was once a piece of me
will be a piece of him—

But I ask that you keep the
June scented sweaters
the daffodils and the butterfly orchids—
I don't want to be
surreal

I don't want you to regret us
I don't want you to regret…
me

I wish I were more courageous
but I'll leave this note
to let you know

I had no loss of affection,
you and I just weren't meant to be
and unfortunately, our fascinations for one another
weren't—
stimulated by love,
just *infatuation*

But I *promise* that I will hold onto our memories
because I don't know if I will ever find
anyone or anything better
than you

5 01 93

Manhattan

I will never forget *you*
I will never forget
I will never
I will
I…

5 07 93

The Lover

I wish you wouldn't hide behind
what you paint on your face—
because I just want to see you

But instead I am falling in love with
the women that want to be you,

You told me I was 'the one'
but I now understand that
you meant odd,

You weren't used to a romantic

You were used to satisfying your rush
through caging yourself within the walls of
a heartless man's misery

I remember once you
covered my eyes
and said

 "Blinded love is the best kind of love. No longer
can thy eyes be the blame, only thy heart."

I didn't want to
understand—

What you call pain is what I call sacrifice
I gave parts of me, you never *returned*
I was the muse to your voided emotions
and you only showed affection in bravado

I embellished myself through chivalry
as a means to receive what I dreamed for
but you saw it as a weakness
which I found not lessening but weakening

So now I
think of what's next—

Will you spend nights under the city lights
with guys that I know?
And see me dining
with women you don't know?

Will you look at him
and think to yourself
"this isn't it" and wish that
it was me
you were with

For you I was a gentleman
for you I was a lover
for you I was a poet
for you I was a romantic

For you I was what
shooting stars wish for

And for me
you were just

a drowning dream
incapable of coming true

Rosetta

I hear your voice behind me
you're cold
but still— angelic
Rosetta

Look how far
apart we've grown
Rosetta

Do you remember
the *poems for you*
Rosetta

You were "My Cleopatra, my last"
Rosetta

But after *me*
you became
their summer *mornings*
their winter nights
Rosetta

No more fading
handprints on the windows
only lip printed innuendos
from other women

I used to
love you
but now we are
DiMaggio and Monroe
Rosetta

I told you I feared
I was losing you
when you were chasing
the life

Rosetta now
we will never know how far
we could have gotten together

Now you're just a poem
inside of my book
Rosetta

This wasn't the way
our future was suppose to look
Rosetta

But I have a secret and
one last stanza for you
Rosetta

In the *beginning*
this was all for *you*

Rosetta…

5 07.93

I'll be fine

Hold on
Hold on
I need you to stay

All this time I didn't listen
when you felt something was missing
and that your touch would *turn* to dust
with the time

Reaching for you
seems like the only thing to do

Because my thoughts are feeling different
and when I'm in this position
eyes can't see what I will be
missing tonight

Runaway *love*
it's okay love
I'll be fine

Lying here with you alive in my mind
even if you *arrived* I'll know you're not mine

But I'll be awake when
other women come around
less modest
less you

Then I'll sleep with
subtle sounds

I know they'll never be *enough*
but I'll be fine

Because I know what not
being enough—
feels like

5.07.93

Forrest Affair

Fog swims around
her ankles

The moss lies *asleep*
beneath chipped rocks
cuddled in the morning's dew

She whispers as she walks
the slower
the better

The trees block the sunlight
from reaching the ground and
the leaves on the branches
kick the warm light
back up to the skies

Vines grace the soles of her feet
mist from the nearby waterfall
creates a haze
around her and me

I place
a hand on her hip and another
on the back of her neck, and draw her
closer to me
feeling the scent of maple and rose
run in my nose

Her cheeks press my own,
She whispers to me
"We are two lovers of the same cause
except I spring and you fall "

I hear her—

I kiss her, I wanted
to feel Juno's *fear*—
Juno's *love*
for the last time
until the next time

The sunlight gushes past the trees
crawling to sleep in the fallen leaves
the smell of cedar and bark surrounds me
her whispers become voices in my mind
figments of my disposition

Maybe I could have called her back to me
but what would I say?
she creates
and I decay

But I'm content
because I know
she'll be *back again*
and that's the best part about

missing her

Pearl

Inside the heart of the beast
on wheels of brimstone
with my mistress *Pearl*
hailing from under seas
dressed in silk, sunken
in the tear ducts of the pacific soil

We arrive—

Her feet hit
the red carpet
igniting the tongue
to flames
I hear the screams,
yet I step deep into the flame as well.

An island of lights—

The cameras capture, the essence of her:
the red tint in her diamond rings
the curves in her dress

Impatient romancing—

She grabs my fedora
and places a soft kiss,
on my cheek
rushing her hands down my
chest as I grab to feel
what the heart cannot.

Bouquet of memories

We smile, as the
lenses gaze at us
we have never felt
this alive—
this *young*
before

It's always ephemeral

With each flash
I feel a past part of me
thicken—
and fall
disappearing into the
red tongue

Pain is *melodic*, too

She enjoys this
and graces a smile

5 07 93

Cold Fridge Magnet

Dear *Pearl*—
I can't do this,

All you propose
to do is argue

You praise yourself
for succumbing to
all that you perceive
to be pristine

You are
numb with indifference

The words you brew bruise
"restless" minds
like mine

You always tell me
"You're a step behind"

But
how many steps behind
do you think I need to be to leave you?

I smothered emotion with
the living room pillows
tied regret to the linen
of the study room carpet

and left prints of relief
on the door knob,

Find your way out
of this one

Ravens

My eyes turn to stones
of black and white
while gazing at the
broken pieces of porcelain
grabbing the spiral ceramic tiles
into monogamy

Where is my
Lenore?

With instrument
in hand
scratching lead
on *torn* pieces
of papyrus
I write

"Moonlight is only
a lonesome lover in heaven's illustrious lamp
shining her ominous lantern
to lure me; she knows I'm an aesthete"

Angels whistle to me
from behind the windows
gusts of wind clap against the
wooden roof

I do not hear *Lenore*

out there
I fear a *raven*
is near

But I must get back to my work
no more distraction
I will continue
scratching lead
on *torn* pieces
of papyrus
with Paul moving
my hands
and Saul covering my eyes

"She is here for me,
where are you *Lenore?*"

Veni Vidi Perdidi

Maybe the euphoria
was tasteless

My utopian goddess—
I crowned myself with
your presence
and crowned you
with their praises

You spoke avalanches of love
but I melted them into
your tears
and the streams showed
they flowed like the Nile

I wish they flowed regularly
the other way—
I wish they were mine instead

I ask for your forgiveness
but I speak in harmonious horror
melodic insignificance

I'm sorry for making my uncertainties
sound so persuasive
I'm sorry for disguising them
as pillars for our future

Is he better than me?

He probably is
he knows and has what he wants

He has you,
I had you

You loved me,
you love him

We don't speak anymore
and this will probably continue
we won't speak anymore

Just remember

That night in Georgetown,
the last time I saw you
the last time I had a chance
the last time I walked away from you
the last time you ran after me
the last time you cared
the last time I felt you
the last time I could have…

The last night—

5 07 93

Beyond The Glass, Charlie

You know Charlie—
glass windows tend to
give them a sense of
security
a sense that may
easily be confused with
protection,

But see Charlie
they shouldn't
stand behind glass windows
not because they may be seen
but because of what is
beyond the glass

The danger

For them the glass window
not only serves as a mental barrier
but it also serves as their sight of *perception*
their sight of
what is out there

The danger

The sad thing Charlie

is that they don't know how to see
they don't know what to look for

The danger

but if they knew of
the danger,
they wouldn't really need
windows...
would they Charlie?

5.07.93

Genesis

Legacy begins
after the book is closed,
when the message has
to move on to the next legend

You're given a spark
in a world of darkness

You can choose to run from what you have been
given
and become just another faded sound
in the chorus of time

Or you can choose to scorch the skies with your
passion
and watch the flames fall
and *beautify* the world

You
are the only hope

You—
the one who was
once a reader
turning pages in the dark
unaware of what you were to become

But then
there was light

5.07.93

Helen

The strings of her violin
shook the Berlin walls
into life's debris

Volumes of her story
screech in the rubble
sounding her secrets
sounding her longing
seeping into the cities soil
stealing its riches

Her satin dress
her veil
her silk knitted cuffs
sown in Munich
her pearl's coral white glow
her wrists blazing lights of silvers
complementing the gold
chaining her fingers in beauty

When I'm here with her, her sounds are all that
exist
allowing her and I to coexist in melodic
nothingness
a lover's euphoria

Winter's Eden
she freezes my heaven, to a blizzard's dream
and I can wait
for the warmth to settle

But if it never does

I will
listen to Helen,
play her sorrow
to me
for my *eternity*

5.01.93

Liquid Disposition

I.

I lie where footprints are embedded and
dig my fingers into the pond

But as I lift my hand the
water runs back into the pond

II.

I spread my fingers and drop
them into the pond

Twirling them inside the pond
dancing them inside the pond
pulling them out of the pond
but the water runs back

I ball my fists and bang them
inside of the pond
causing ripples
but the ripples soon vanish

III.

The sun brings warmth to my back
and the pond

I place my hands inside the pond

I pull my hands out
and the water runs back into the pond

The pond evaporates

I sob for years
and there lies another pond

IV.

She lies where footprints are embedded

she digs her fingers into the pond

5 01 93

Paris

You burn the eager tongue in me
twirl where seasons turn to leave
my— ever loving queen
seen through shuttered eyes
you say to love is wise
and that regret is just fallen kin
to the son of time

You vacate my cluttered mind
and keep safe my inner Zion
you escape within my eyes only to
blow kisses that I see floating
on the wings of butterflies

I've been told
to chase is foolish
and time consuming,
and that
I may never catch what I'm pursuing
but I'd rather try than never know
because
you're the only thing that seems tangible
in both reality
and my dreams

I don't see why
I should ever let you go

5.07.93

1993

Age seems to bitter
life's nectars

Memory fades—
following in youth's footsteps
only to be captured in Polaroid film

New generations
replace the past ones

They're new,
we're old

Our Saturday morning cartoons
have forgotten us

They have new—
friends

We can no longer follow the yellow brick road
with Judy Garland

Our steps are no longer
needed

Our napping adventure lands
forbid our return

We've lost our

means of entrance
we've lost our innocence

And sadly
it seems that soon
we'll fade
following in memory's footsteps
only to be captured in digital pixels

Life is just a cycle

5.01.93

Nagasaki

I never thought the imagined
would begin, inside a place
with walls such as these.

I walk past the receptionist
down hallway tiles marked
by skirted wheels
that had to perform sharp turns
into a room of life cords where
time takes rest and
the ending speaks
in a language of beeps.

"Who are you?"
you ask.

I whisper to you,
"Any brick picked up on
memory lane is a detour."
Your face lights up like a July sky.

Why are you smiling?
Is it coming back now?

Do you remember how your yellow daisy flannels
brushed against my corduroys

and the ocean
in 1945?
It was mid—day and
I remember because that's when
the gulls designed the skyline
and when the sunlight hit the
high tides— making them mirror
rolling bridges of fire.

We ran in the soft palms of the sand.
As we looked back, you said you forgot
which footprints were your own.

Well, I knew my prints from yours—
I just never told you.
I figured it was one less thing
for you to forget.

To me
you were no more at your prime then
than you are now.
Still just as beautiful,

Although the streams of life in your hands
do not flow as warm as before

And your brown—streaked hair
is still as celestial

but now white as winter
patched snow.

But you wouldn't remember
any of this.
You never could have,

You probably didn't remember
the events of that *night*
the following *morning*

All of my romancing,
lost in your *memory*

(Hearing the sound of
feet behind the door)

"But I must go now,
I must, and oh I brought you
Lilacs— your favorite...
the nurse laid them by your bed."

You whisper,
"No, tell me more of 1945."

I say,
"*I can't begin to tell you.*
Just remember

I'd call you Nagasaki
and you'd call me Bing Crosby."

"Who are you?"
you ask.

I whisper to you,
"Any brick picked up on
memory lane is a detour."
Your face lights up like a July sky.

5.01.93

Bed of Lights

Knit my dreams
no—

Weave them on your loom
into the star—lands

Maybe then they'll be
noticeable

Racing through the night
the peninsula in the skies
the *bed of lights*

Their reflection
swimming in your eyes

Floating in the seas
following your essence
to the harbors
to safety

Pharos of
Alexandria

I want to
share them—

I want to
share this

With *you*

Your love
and wonder
are what will
keep them—

Are what will
keep *us*

Together

Are you going
to stay
this time?

I don't want
to be dream catcher
again

5.01.93

The Potomac

There is a French coffee mug,
overflowing with Green Tea
on a Swedish breakfast coaster
in the lobby

I *left* it
there

I figured I'd leave
a piece of me behind
just in case you decided
to show up,

I *know* it's
over—

Maybe these green leaves
are making me naïve

5.01.93

Unattainable

My staccatos
weren't enough

Blame me for
my inconsistency

You called
me "romantic" —

I failed to live up to that
I fell short
while falling for you

My Maryland charm
wasn't enough for your
New York winds

I regret the last night in Virginia
the inactions
the hesitations

You were ready
and I wasn't

I made the night *forgettable*—
for you
while you gave me a night to remember
even through your subtleties—
you *cared*

You wanted—

you wanted…

Maybe me and Rod
shouldn't have fallen asleep
so early that night

Maybe I was afraid
of disappointing

Maybe I thought there would
be more opportunities—
more nights

Maybe you were
right

But we'll
never know—

And if you ever forget me
I'll understand

Just promise me that
you will never forget
the lights

5 01 93

Attainable

Blue Jays sing the *mornings* to you—
the cherry blossoms' *adolescence*
the *language* of the sun

The Iroquois named
their river after your *essence*—
Ohio

The winds carry the voices of angels
singing in heavenly laced legatos for you
in balladic beauty

I am no Blue Jay
I am no Iroquois
and I am no angel

But I am your
lover
and
My ode to you,
is lettered in the life I live

5 01 93

Sequence 1

DREAM

The World of the Drifter

Above the
realm of existence

Where thoughts graze sleep
where daydreams reside

A land of no fears and close tribes
even with diversity
pain can hide here

Without its
masks—

Here we emote what we feel
so we may find what we seek
and escape loneliness

Here we cherish friendships
and arts
which accompany us for now and after
replacing endowment with laughter

Here we live in—

A world where freedom rings
and is *heard*

A world where lovers interact
with one another

A world condoned by the bigger picture
the world known only by the people of peace
and The Drifter

5.01.93

Eve

A summer's eve
under the skies

Spend time with me
knowing that you will never get it back

Follow me through the forests
through the prairies
through the fields of daffodils

Wonder by the lake of dreams
with me

See my reflection in its
waters

Tell me what you think
of me

Tell me what you think
of my dreams

5.01.93

Remember

Sweet memories fade
apart from every gaze
at what we once were

My hands used to grasp
your pronounced curves
and brush against
the bliss in between
the streams of pain we conquered
together

You told me
I would have to wait
but— my distaste
for your recent absence
has caused me to wonder
if you're counting until eternity
to give me
what you say I deserve

I don't know if I can wait that long
how can a mortal lover—
keep an immortal promise?

Please forgive me if my impatience gets the best of
me
but how long is forever?

You promised me you were coming back remember?

5 07 93

Dreamland

Guitars, cellos
Apollo's lyre
enchanted by evergreen petals
breeding sweetened melodies—
echoes of nature

The moon glooms
afar in the sky
stars lie on a open plain
spaciously widening

Fields— alive with
tulips and orchids
blossoming as the
world swirls in marvelous color

Blue jays and eagles
dream in the starlight
flying across the see—through skies

Oceans clear to the absolute
bottom

Beautiful beasts indulge in hibernation
fierce mammals wander gracefully

Whales blow water in the air
to be lit by the light of the moon

making each particle of liquid
a mirror

Skylines are soaked
 in the moon's silver

Gravity of the mind
holds all in place
here

Welcome to the land where
time and I
share words

Welcome
my dreams

Where
I am forever a day old

Bow & Arrows

It's early June and
I still pinch myself
when you speak to me

We chase Cupid with his own
arrows together

Until we realize
the power—
of the arrows

You stare at me
while the last arrow
is held between my fingers
and the bow

You whisper
"aim for the heart"

I awake

5 07 93

Jack the Bear

Can't you see that
you're not invisible man

Does it evade you
and take shelter
within the pockets of your pants
is it in shades you cannot
apprehend

Well the clock ticks again
can you stop this again
or give in
and feel the shock

Jack you can't

Change is now
it begins

There's no going back
to the Chthonian
you hear me Jack?

It's time to leave
the hole you're in

Cold bourbon and precarious faces
will only keep you running

in directions against your own will
aren't you tired of running Jack?

If you stay in the darkness
you'll just stay a machine Jack
a living machine
are you a machine Jack?

You have your own thoughts
you have your own mind
you can think Jack

You are not a machine—

I know you've
been in darkness for awhile now
but eyes can readjust Jack

And as the readjustments are made
everything will— feel more real.

You are no Barbee
you have the ability to see
the ability of sight
use it Jack

And let "free" the suitcase too
come back to reality
let identity find you

no more complaining or crying Jack
make the most of this life my friend

You don't have to worry about
Ras and Brother Jack
anymore

The Brotherhood proved to be an illusion
and nothing more
than another place to run
to and from…

Mary Rambo kept you warm and safe
she made you feel like a child again
but she couldn't awaken
your mind to a state of consciousness
only you could

You've been through a lot
and all of these different events
make you who you are
so how can you still remain
invisible?

You are— and forever will be
created in his image

Let you heart be
your mirror

You will never be invisible
as long as you can see yourself

5.07.93

Mist in May

I'm lost

All I hear is her voice
in the mist

Directed by something
invisible to my eyes,

I'm prone to guard myself
and resist to feel her,

But this has never happened before,
and it may never happen again

But why mingle with what
the eye cannot see?

The same reason why I breathe to fill my lungs
with something unseen—

In hope of
remaining

I'm falling for her
getting lost for her

Is falling alone better than being alone?

Then again

She's lost

All she hears is a voice
in the mist

Directed by something
invisible to her eyes

Rosso Fiorentino

Red Florentine
a wielder of luxurious oils
and frescoes

A mannerist,
compelled by
and the hand's incentive
to create

In excess gratitude
I thank you
for *Angelo Musicante*
a piece synonymous
to a metonymy
of emotion through sounds
that find words useless

Your ability is one
that is rarely tamable

An ability that is
timeless
an ability I wish
to hone
as soon as I can find it
within myself

5 01 93

The World of the Drifter II

Freedom of the mind
bred by everlasting opportunities
moments of inspiration
and romance

Allowing me to drift off to
a space
composed by pain
and love

Here
flickers of life graze
the skies
and tears land in the fists
of the stars

Here,
dreams are saviors
and are all that are savored
by my belief
which never wades

Until I'm awakened to leave
until I'm awakened to stale truths

Where they tell me who I can be—
who I can't be
where people trade their dreams
for materials

But vivid memories remind

Of the freedom that awaits me

Creating sweetness within the bitter—
preserving serenity

Until I'm delivered to rest
until I'm processed to slumber

Then memories will no longer be needed
because all that was remembered through memory
will return
and all that returns
will be peace, love
and everything a Drifter could ever dream of

Sequence 2

NIGHTMARES

Romancing Tongues

To wonder—
a sensual haunting

An invisible note
in the heart's ballad
played in silenced sounds
sounding in its tongue—
wonder is language

What wondrous
thoughts
what wondrous
dreams

Wonder—

what a gown to wear
on thy self
on thy mind
on thy life

What a wonderful gown
to keep thee warm
to keep thee cloaked
to keep thee safe

Wonder
what a wonderful
escape
what an everlasting breath

To know—
what a beautiful adventure
to remember and soon forget
knowing the lights in the skies
only brighten the sound of the voices
falling from the clouds—
knowledge is language

Eve's desire
a swim in dreamless waters
a mountain with a peak
but without elevation

What a known
tomorrow

What a road—
with an end

5 07.93

The Time I Have Wasted

I walk on the
debris of time

I am terrified at what I find—
unfulfilled promises and
memories that live in tears
which I fear are mine

You see
I'm where the immaculate hears and heals the blind
but I feel nothing

The days are crimes but the years are fines,
I see no path; I'm scared the lines prepare what
repairs my mind
but the lines come to an end, at the last period
and I'm not ready for the climax

Time's lines only move forward
even when I live in the past
I still age—
I've never been young

I clench vines of faith for
the sake of my darkest ages
and stutter when I think of being a remark in
between the lines of a heartless author's final pages

From where I stand, this maze
continues to make understanding— a hopeless
dream
there seems to be no entrance or exit

My spirit, even when its sense is scarce, cherishes
both what I *live* off of and *perish* from

Past heartache moans as it sleeps behind me
and its melody enchants me as I hear it
in—between my failures and merits
so I do not bury the heartache
but add on to its melody
moving skies with the stroke of a pencil

Which constitutes the basis for why
apologies become a part of me

The writing, isn't satisfying
but I still continue to make
the most of what I have been through

The people need this
I hear will in their voices
I see it in their faces

They feel the need to feed off of the
time I have wasted

5 07 93

French Rose

The auburn scarf
the scarlet brooch
the amber stoned necklace

The firebrick sweater
the jasper hairpin
the denim jacket

The pastel paintings
the wool carpets
the marble floors

The candlelight—
in the dining room

The rose petals—

The first time you
told me

The last time
I saw you

5.07.93

June Blues

(To the waitress)

May I have a
cup of magma?

I think I'm thirsty
I hope this helps me
I got the blues
everyone has left me
except for you

Pour another
and another

You know this drinking
is only temporary
you know your waiting
is only temporary

But none of that matters
right now
does it

Pour another
and another

I know what you're thinking

"Sad man, he's trying to see
through teary eyes"

But you are wrong
I'm not trying to see

Pour another
and another

I'm trying to have
this magma

I just want to hear the blues
that's all I want

What's that you ask
why do I consume magma?

I don't consume the magma
the magma consumes me

You see I'm just a figment of
the magma
it is blues
and blues is me
I am magma

Pour another
and another

Maybe they'll all come back
maybe everyone will return

They need me don't they?

Pour another
and another

 You need me don't you

Pour another
and another

I'm ready for the June blues
I'm ready to play the June blues

You don't have to pour anymore
I've had enough, just listen and

Indulge in me

Fame

Rain pour becomes
heavenly melodic
when *alone*

Promises un—kept
seem to be pardoned
by the rains and their *roars*

Their love—
their *cheers*
their praises—
pantomime my life

And I don't know
what I will do
when they're gone

When the skies stop
letting them go

I don't know what
I will do…

5 07 93

Sequence 3

BLISS

Venice

(Music plays in the ballroom)

An emerald jewel
on her necklace

Her beauty
a sleeping monsoon

Being young—
I want what my eyes see

Beauty is in the eye of the beholder
and I need to hold her
in order to feel the landscape of perfection

I am entranced by
the starry sky
in her dress

The lights
shower my eyes

I walk to her and compliment
her as she compliments me

I can sense her character
in her voice
joyous— lovely
mysterious

I can see suspense
spinning around her
and the axis is love

Her goddess appeal
Aphrodite's only competition

Time is slipping away
the last song is near its end

But I'm
in no rush

Our night's youth
has only just begun

5 01 93

Happiness Galore

Faith and grace
grab and taste
understand— embrace
spread your hands to feel,
smile and relate

Praise and rejoice
express peace,

Remember to always
believe in yourself

Follow your heart
never let your mind and will
be apart

Let forever
be your start

Plan before you proceed
stand before you walk
pay no attention to enemies
survive through the darkness

Let your all be the one and only thing
you ever bring

Allow inspiration to flow on the wind
as you talk always stay above it all

never will you drop
never shall you stop

Earn and own everything for which you fought for
attain what you sought for

Soar to
heaven's doors
ring the bells
end wars

Watch for the future generations
make sure that they will have more
than you could ever ask for

Influence and restore
be a savior— support
help the poor
and poorer

Failure is
something you cannot afford

Let the
glory rattle the floor

Live and explore

Make paths— open doors

and make sure you'll be the first
through but not the last

Work while others sleep
hurt— but never encounter defeat
aim high and let the clouds
hold up your feet

Keep correct health, never frail nor weak
conquer obstacles astronomical

Quench the dry and defeated,
with happiness

Bring all who love with peace
together

Stay victorious
this destiny is yours
this is happiness galore

Prague

The love of my dreams
here before me
in the form of life

Reality inspired by
my heart's imagination
the *art* of God's creation

You breathe
life into me
and I do the same
for you
the beauty of –
miracle

Although the cage
inside
is there to protect

It allows me in
so my beat can match yours

Faith's keys seek locked doors
in hope of unlocking
happiness

Trust me
if you let me in
I'll unlock yours

You're all I ever thought for
the reason *for my being*
love binds you and I together
our feelings run beyond time

Since we're going to last forever
there is no need to worry
only to remember

88's Love Song

In early morning

When eyes open
sensation is burning

Music sheets lie
on my chest
awaiting sound

In sympathy I stroke the keys
to emote *harmonic* ventilation

Healing
the aimless echo
the colorless thought

Playing off *bare* memory and
naked fear

Entertaining memories of
retrospect from
last night's revelry

The black and white noise *blends*
in all sense of matrimony

The bond of the waves
that ripple before my eyes

Is invisible—

But since I play with my
eyes closed
and my heart *open*

I don't need to see it
it is love in the form of song

I feel it

Ballad to the Heart

I play for her heart—
as unbelievable as that sounds to you
just imagine how it sounds to her
it is truth

She feels the eager life in me
through black and white keys

They give me a winning chance
they allow me to allure her
they are my instruments of *romance*

5.07.93

Fireworks in September

I remember
Time took rest
to watch our last breaths
of romance

We were both young
the rush of warmth and
our youth—
together

I'd hold you until
our hearts would beat as one
and I'd listen as
you'd whisper in my ear
that I was the only one
for you

My eyes
would run
all over your body
and plunge into an abyss of
your love
in hope of never reaching the bottom

I miss
the *everlasting* grasp
of your lips on mine
and how the sunshine would
illuminate your hair

in such a beautiful hue
and how your aroma walked on the
air that the wind blew
around us
where only love surrounded us
there love had found us

And although those days
have passed
and will never come again
the memories are still alive
September will never end

5 07 93

You

You allow me to smile
my diamond in the rough
no matter how much I give to you
I know that it will never be enough

You deserve the world
and all the good that is in it

I know I can fill up the atmosphere
with all the feelings
that I have for you

Where you walk the flowers bloom
you make the fires yield
you heal my inner wounds

It seems that I can only use clichés
these days
but luckily you don't care much for them
because out of all of the words that I say
only three of them matter

You are always perfectly groomed
in my eyes
I just hope you can see
how important you are—
soon

So that you can return to the good
and resume
keeping all that's worth saving
safe

I hope that you keep
a second to realize that
you're the very reason I stay

When I feel lonesome
you bring me back
you keep me calm

My love will always be attainable
for you

Even when no one cares

And please know
I'd never let you go through anything
that you could not bear

And I hope that you will always remember
that in the dark
when you are alone
I will be there
to show you that
you're the light

And in this day and forever
it's you and me, together

so however
or whenever
times get harder
just know
that you will never
be alone

5 07 93

Ms. New Yorker

The perfect moments
always seem to pass away
before I get a chance
to tell you what
I have to say

But If I told you
in a different way
would it mean the same
and would I still be the man
that you want me to be

If what you want from me
is what you say you need
then honestly
I believe it may be what I need too

And now I know I cannot leave
because I do not want this to be
our last memory together—
this may be the
last chance that I will ever have
to see you

So I can't let anymore of
these moments pass

I want you to notice

everything you have ever wanted
is what I have always had

Winter whispers baby blue
in favor of *us*
whistling our ballad in white snow—
give *us* a chance

Trying could never be
pointless—
these feelings pierce so deeply

I hope that you feel them too
because the *oxeye daisy* is running
out of petals

5 07 93

Us

Heartfelt melodies
and your fearlessness
are what allow me to be
your soul's connoisseur

Apart from being a friend to me
you are my mating soul
you are my bliss in its entirety
and I believe
the life inside of me—
cannot rely on me anymore

It relies on you
it lies in us
it lives in me
but it is alive in us

5 01 93

Toronto

When our world spins
And flickers in black and white
The features of my fears come to life

Passion lit up in a fire
Without *hue*

Is the emblem
Of my desire without you

You are the love of my *color*
In shades invisible without
The touch of light

5 01 93

Spring of '98

The dew slept in the
wealth of the soil

How old was I?
I believe 5

Too young to understand the
sight of Mother Nature
nurturing the life deep within my eyes

Closed eyelids could not shelter
the beauty of nature's innocence

Neither could my hands block the golden
rays of the sun

An attempt foolish yet memorable
but soon enough I drop my hands
and open my eyes

A cascade of color
a collage of insurmountable beauty

I remember watching the skies shed tears to
nourish the land
while the sun was still heating the skin
of the forests
each drop completing an unforgettable phase
resembling that of the change from a crescent to a

full moon

I have no photo
to prove this remarkable setting
and also I am in no regret

 I rather
allow the image to
forever—last within
my memory
and yours

5 07 93

Sequence 4
Lifemare

The Last Sight

"I want something lasting and unpredictable,
something infinite and complete."

He had heavy eyes, with a tight nose
his leather jacket clung to his skin
as if it were a part of him

During the night
he would take strolls alone—
accompanied only by light poles

In between moments of silence
his eyes would lower and stare at the icy rivers
the same river where he learned how to swim,

the same river where he last saw her

He remembers
how lovely life used to be

But on this night much would change
it would become his most memorable stroll

After wiping tears of regret
he lifted his head
and glided on the snow patched road

As the night chilled
he watched snowflakes melt on the air he blew
and left prints of angels in batches of snow
hoping to relive what he knows
will never return

Then he wounded up in a yarded area
on the field of the extinct
there he showed
gratitude to those
he seemed to outgrow

He believed luck
was beyond gracious to him

When it became time to leave
he stuck

his finger up for guidance
but the wind did not blow
the gusts were stilled

He squinted
beyond the street's ever stretching lanes
he saw what appeared to be a door near
the snow angel imprints
and he became perplexed

It could just be a mirage
at its unremitting core
he thought

The man ran swiftly
forgetting his luck
at the field

He expressed much excitement as he
grew closer to what his eyes
failed to piece together

As he reached the end of the lane
his existence poured
seeping into the angel snow

There he had found what he was
looking for …

A Perfect Life

A man slowly decomposing himself
in the false permanence of a fast life
misunderstanding that
unlike the richness of the soul
a man's lustful desires falter and lose
value as each year goes by
rapidly becoming, nothing more
but perennial blurs in life's memorabilia

But his unawareness protected his ignorance
he lived without remorse
he had no wife of course
just picked women without caution
only remembering those
who managed to hurt him

And all others who offered love
where left to love alone

He took women around the world
extracting locations from their dreams
spending nights in houses near the
sand painted shores
there was no spot on the planet he had not
explored,

Himalayas and the Andes—
but without family

he longed for a lasting mate
and he would often ponder
but to him contemplation
was an empty disposition

He had no offspring to keep him calm
no one to see
himself in

He visited country's in need
and gave them treasures— but he did not stay

He visited the grandiose lands of the flourished
the lavish suites, in time became his common place
of rest

One bed room suites
no one to sleep with
no one to wake up to
no one to have

Always—
one pillow
too much

He knows he
does not want to live
life alone
he would rather have love

than the luxuries of the world
but no one will ever know
until he allows someone in

Until he decides whether he wants
to give himself to someone
or lose himself to nothing

5 01 93

Man of Dawn

Look into the depthless glow of his eyes
in their swims his demise
racing his hope
near the edge of his pupils

The skies are his halo
the ground is his shackles
he is neither perfect nor inadequate
neither praised nor misunderstood

Just a man containing thoughts
of meaning
a man that knows what he has
but is uncertain of what he wants
a man with little time to decide
his purpose

A man of Dawn

5 07 93

The Artist

It is 3 a.m.

The piano keys
are stroked with subtleness
and passion
as if this routine
was one
done religiously

The black notes
chill the bones as the music spills
from the heart
from the lungs
to the medium of life
to the invisible words on the mirror
to emotion

No words escape the throat
they escape the mind
and into the microphone soul—
serenity

Cold sounds are bled
effort causes sweat
to swarm above
the skin of him
the skin of the air
the skin of the walls

Breaking breaths
are taken
as he creates

alone

5 01 93

Messenger Boy

Dash

Sealed—
the envelope is between
the grip of my hands
(shaking)

I'm running to deliver
a message

Chasing seconds
in the grip of time's hands—
(steady)

Dash

It is for a patient man
a friend of mine

I think
this news
will heal him

The joy will return,
He will feel
again

The ink she lettered it with
is still wet
I can see it

bleeding out of the envelope
black rose— in color

Dash

I hope she wrote
it clearly
he's been waiting
for *too long*

But what if—
never mind

Dash

5 01 93

Fountain of Gold

He says
"respect my aspiration"

He follows his heart
into the woods
into the dark
into the cave
he knows the allegory

He has immortal desires
with mortal brevity

He wants a fountain of divinity
he would give his waters to Ponce de León
to have his name uttered
to have his name remembered

He wouldn't sell his soul—
or follow a witch's prophecy
he isn't Faustus
he isn't Macbeth

He is a man
one among many—
he is evanescent

He searches bliss—
but will it cause him to
become addicted to perfection?
Will he become dependent upon believing
he can mimic the glimmering silvers

of a winter night?

Will he see as Midas did
and learn that once gold
isn't as valuable as love
and the nectars of life?
Marigold's statue

That is a risk between heaven and regrets grip
but he's still willing to take it
he may lose everything on the way towards
reaching what he wants
but he doesn't care
he just wants to make it there

5 01 93

V.

I hear heart's beating
around me
excited—
wanting

But none of them
sound familiar

None of them sound like
the sound behind your chest
that your words couldn't make

My heart beats for that sound
I breathe for that sound
and I fear my last beats
and my last breaths
begin to approach
whenever I think of that sound
finding harmony
without me

In response to loneliness
I make symphonies
with others
not out of love
but out of despair

we sound together, it is never love
it is never for them—

A lone wolf
eats alone

I know I haven't changed
but I can—

But you have to come back—
I won't waste my youth
waiting for you

Until my hope fades
I will continue to be
love's martyr

But

Until your familiar sounds return
I will continue to listen to theirs—
and add on

It's only fair—

5 01 93

Werewolves

Heart half empty
and glasses half full
the poison was so plenty
and his past so cruel

He tells them

"It is loudest
when everything is quiet

Breaths seem to ring the ears
and linger there
stares speak— in volumes
whispers ripple and roll on the neck
down the chest
down the spine

Sounds of silence
falling fabrics, leathers, furs
and lightless bedrooms

Glut is followed by rush
wrapped in the covers of
the bed
and time is spent for pleasures
seeming to last forever
until the morning light"

They listen—
and then they begin

As a pack
in the night
wolves of Aphrodite
wolves of seduction
consuming his once
passionate life

He wants this
he wants them

He can't help himself
and they can't help him

5 01 93

Memphis Blues

To him
love is dry

So he sinks his veins in the damp
sands of revelry
just to stay hydrated

He says

"Love is just
a heartless woman
with burning beauty—
lighting dreams to flames
while laughing
with the residue of a past man's love
crying in her breathe

There is no love for me"

5.01.93

The Leader

Gorilla warfare
is all that is considered war here

Money is never seen but it
always pours here
but in the form of
bullets, machines
and nuclear deposits

Even after courageous acts are committed
for the people—
soldiers don't exist
just the chief and the depth
of the wealth in his pockets

He is chief
but he is a man who can't
remember the rights of truth

He is a chief
but he's a man accustomed to brutality
a man who is a lothario

You all call him leader?

But you have no idea
where he is going to lead you
and he has all the knowledge of what
he is leading
but he has no knowledge of where
he is to lead

So he claims assurance
when all is unknown and hidden
within the mystics of his confusion

His smiles burn holes in his
followers curiosities
they cannot see the hypocrisy

They cannot see that
his laws, ideals and customs
are all unidentifiable when naked

They cannot see
that this is all an illusion

5.01.93

A Night Story

The street signs—
speak "stop"

Lights breeze
rose red
but the brake pedal
is never touched

The suede seats
are never embraced with
a print of fear

Pale tires turn
in red speed motion—
screeching on the pavement
while gliding across the
yellow and white lines

The windows begin to slide down
imitating the roof

The gold in her hair
sets the air to blaze
his heart—
like fire
thumping in
flickering sounds

Eyes contact one another
triggering a smile
a night long adventure is
what they are now living for

As if life
lasts a night

The thrust of one body on another
as the soul gasps for air
a climax, followed by another—
and another,

All of this
done before the
breaking of day

A night— worth living

Again

5.07.93

The Last Time

She has already put three people
that you know to rest

Right in front of you
only seconds ago

Yet you still want your
chance at taste

You want her
more than anything

More than anything...

Watch as she unfolds for you
blowing out the smoke from
the love pistols

Time your final glances wisely
as you take your last look at her
through the windows of the
revolver as it spins

Capture this *moment*

Because it will
never happen
again

Bang...Bang—
Bang

Third time is
the *charm*

5.07.93

Black Ink Delirium

At the snap of a finger
shake of salt and pepper
minds infect
the dialect
born on a fighter's breath
to make one believe
the return of
Malcolm X to Mecca

But that is not make believe
its Afrocentric,
like the reminiscence
of the hole in a pocket
in wonder of where lost cents went
or like peace
held within the cheeks
of a Buddhist monk
chewing on morality
to survive

Self—reliance at times
is self—purification
these lines are mere proof
believe me
or make it a belief
because regardless
this truth resembles
those affected by
Stalin's purges
carried out by his merciless workmen
in his mind dissolving service

Do not panic
now that propaganda
and reality mated
and created
the illusion of self—security
you can disown the
lies
and grow a disaffection
for the hallucinations
that the voices on screens
and radios
give you

But if you're not
careful
with what you now know

It will all go
POOF
you understand that,
right?

Well, you have time to
think about this
it is our little secret
you can keep it

Just don't forget to
write me back

5 07 93

Flammable Desire

Young and benign
a selfless learner
at his peak
problematic to the street
where barreled pistols stir
constantly cooking on
crooked curbs
romanticizing with the weak

John heard
this life was bleak
when inside of his older brother's car
resting on cotton seats
watching his older brother
pull out the
ganja from the glove department
placing it on his lap
and digging in his pockets for something
to spark with

(Seconds later
he got the lighter)

"there's no key to relief"
his older brother sung
"but this is something to unlock it"

His older brother inhaled
till the smoke flew from
the windows to the sun
and till his eyes drooped
to his chin
like a Terrier's tongue
he continued to inhale
until he took rest and
parked his car
as he said " I'm tired little one"
wake me up when the moon desires what its won"

Jack watched his older brother slip to slumber
and picked up the refiner like a crumb
and puffed slowly
and began coughing as he
let it
burn fire in his lungs

He breathed in and blew out
without knowing it could kill his
entire rebuttal to a struggle
without knowing it was
a soul blinder

He was weakening his health
and defeating himself
for the sake of his
flammable desire

5.07.93

Sequence 5

LONER

Growing Up

Will you be there
at my hour of sorrow
when all hope points to
flowers above me tomorrow?

This may be the last portrait
so paint this picture vividly
color me patiently, with calm hands
and paint my heart large in the center

Do you remember how I would smile
understanding the comedy of life—
like *The Comedian* from *Watchmen*?

But now I reminisce, cynical and defeated
sitting in the
coldest winds failures and warmth

Speak to me
please— tell me you will stay
through the rough blows of thunderous impassions
and anxious grays

I just can't be alone in this locket
of stone and terror

I've grown away from my peers
and what I now hear
is that everyone has moved on
and forgotten how we
grew up with each other
laughed with each other
fell in love with each other
fell out of love with each other
missed each other—
and left each other

You're all I have left

Grow up with
me for a little while longer

Passive

I forgot
please remind me

Don't leave
it is so cold
here

Will you stay young with me?
we can watch time pass and
grow old on us

We can poke holes in the skies
and bathe in the starlight

We can count to forever
and stop at five

We can jump into autumn's leaves,
and wonder of the lost color—
to see what we will never be

You and I
together

But I forgot
can you remind me?
why do we have to pass away—

5.07.93

Life Goes On

Apart—
a distance rarely understood

Even if you could grasp
the silhouette of what it once was
it would be mistaken as an apparition

You weep, in sorrow
to fill regret
and empty the soul of the eyes

You evoke
words that venture along
parallels of memories
and dreams

You reminisce because of
troubling mementos
and lifelike mares
laced in the space between
the distances

You fear never attaining
what you've lost

You fear this will worsen you
you fear this will lessen you

But maybe it's

better this way

5.07.93

Afternoon

I'm away again

Away from your home
away from you

I never said goodbye
you never said hello

I called last night
I waited
I watched the stars alone

I sounded through
the skies

But I'm not sure
 if you heard me—
the sounds I evoked became subtle
and unreliable

My chest grew tired
of the beat inside of it
because it couldn't
beat on the outside
because it couldn't beat
to reach the
unreachable—

It couldn't beat
to reach you

But did you even
want to hear me?

I wonder
if images of me
came to life on your window
as you watched me leave
this afternoon

I wonder
if you watched me leave

5 07 93

The Morning Of

I wish we would have
watched the skies together
that night

You would have loved it
I would have loved you

I thought of
you today—

I will dream of
you tonight

I dream of you often—
I dream I am running to you and
I always find you
but as I begin to touch you
I awake—
I never make it in time

I could never make it in time
I'm sorry

It seems as if you don't
speak to me anymore during the day
because you await me in my dreams

Often I wonder what
will happen if I run to you
while awake—

Maybe you would smile—
maybe you would look through me
maybe someone has already—
ran to you

He'd probably be best for you
I dream it—
he lives it

I think of
writing you

Again—

I wrote you last week—
you didn't respond

Maybe you never got it
maybe I addressed it wrong
maybe I should send it again—

Maybe you were right
when you told me on the morning
of that summer night
maybe it is pointless

Maybe I should
do as you have
and forget about
us

Montreal

The corks fall beautifully
diving into the carpets

Clear glasses are
filled by
the beverage of the night

Here he stands
with a woman from Montreal
wrapping glut on the walls
placing her lips on his face
leaving *prints of red*

He cannot hold back
the excitement
He is trying to disguise
any longer

He is *not ready* for this to end
that would be too
sudden

And time moves too fast
for him to go back
to the bed
in Toronto
where *she* is waiting for me

The burden of this act
will surely bring that house down

Just for the love

of these seductive women
lipstick stains
and Valentine linen

But why them
over her ?

He is just a man
who doesn't know what he wants

Bravery

I rather not hide within
the dust that falls outside
of the black panther's leather gloves—
which once pointed to the virgin moon
with a fistful of black lineage

I rather not hide within
the microphone that projected
the revolutionary speeches of
Dr. Marin Luther King Jr.
and chauffeured vocals on expressways
leading our ears to the soul of Etta James
At Last black souls reached
bigger dreams

I rather not hide within
the inked pages of
Langston Hughes, Lucille Clifton and
Maya Angelou

I rather show myself,
in humility
I rather show myself
in color
I rather show myself
in solicitude

Because If I do not—
I am *invisible*

Black Coffee

Black coffee
swallowing the Swedish
sugar cubes

The man beside me
speaks to me of his family
in Lithuania
he brushes his nose with
each of his knuckles
as he pulls out photos
of his daughter,
nine years of age
wearing a red ribbon hair pin
and a blue dress
lying in a field of daffodils

"She's beautiful"
I told him

I dig in my pockets
to show him something
of value to me
pushing my fingers to the bottom
racing my fingertips around
the emptiness

"Nothing…?"
he said

I turned away and watched the
Swedish cubes vanish

Autumn's Rose

June 19th

In your synoptic gospels—
I was Bartholomew

I'm watching you ascend into the heavens
without me
I dare not to follow,
I know I do not belong

Also
my journey is still a long one
and I now know I must venture alone
no longer will companionship be my means
of comfort

I believe solitude may be a firm
replacement
but I also fear that
it is the only candidate left

What have we become, but nonexistent
we are no longer the pristine example of
the nature's connection

We have evaporated —
from its lake of love
its lagoon of prosperity

So what should I do with these feelings?

Should I align them to compose lyrics
created basely upon wishful thinking
or should I cause them to disappear

Feelings that were once so valuable,
now so invaluable— as invaluable
as *us*

I gratefully accept your departure
but I cannot cause these feelings to
disappear
or to fade or to diminish
because you have become a part of me
and to detach a part so caged and protected
would be too painful

I cannot do it alone
I cannot stop something you kept alive—
that would be to surreal, my love

You have to take them with you
as you ascend

Relieve me
for the last time

Billionaire wills his fortune to imaginary friend
(This piece is based off of a satire article)

The huckleberries
dry to flinted stones
but I touch them
I grab them
I chew
I wait

I point

I'm glad
it's Harry

I tell him to taste—
He grabs a branch full
and squeezes the nucleic juices
and I watch as they
explode on his taste buds

He tastes flavor
I taste nothing
He tastes joy
I taste nothing

What is taste?
(taste is nothing)

He tells me to cheer up
and Harry promises me
He'll bring more of me
so that we can taste nothing together

He thinks multiplying sadness
equates to prescriptions of relief—
of acceptance

Harry can taste
but sometimes I wish
he would taste alone again

Sometimes I wish he hadn't
imagined me

5.01.93

Fear (Hope)

I'm learning to preserve
everything with meaning
which for me, is relieving
because now everything I'm wanting
is everything I'm needing

Understand that I'm trying to make a change
while struggling,
with the fear of having nothing on the page
because it seems
that all I write about are my problems
so I think I'll have to quit my craft
as soon as I solve them

That means no more confessions
no more using honesty and packages of David
Sunflower Seeds as
Anti—depressants
but maybe this'll be for the betterment of me
or maybe
in the future
I'll look back and say "wrong" is the way I should
have
kept it

The art of wonder is contagious
making what I once never cared for

now something that I'm craving
and to me life moves
faster when I wonder about what it holds

So I hope this *life* I'm after
is a life worth chasing
one that will put an end
to the concreteness of the pain
on my heart beat's pavement

But until I grasp it I will never know
so hopefully I'll catch up with it
before all of this confusion takes a hold of me

And if I ever do
get there
hopefully that *life* will notice me

5 01 93

Fate's Big Mouth

Often, I wonder if
Fate is prone to making mistakes

Is she acclaimed *perfect*
just because people
fear to question
and result to clichés as
"everything happens for a reason"

Is the flawlessness of Fate statistical
or is Fate just someone who is allowed
to interfere without question—

Is Fate blind?

Fate made a mistake
and ruined true love
Fate made a mistake
and ruined organic love

Fate made a mistake '
and ruined our first date

5.07.93

Thieves

I.   Let's runaway
camp in the seas
and drown

Drowning together
so we won't have to be
the thieves of each other's air anymore

Let's not dip our toes
to feel whether it's hot or cold
let's not try to see the bottom
let's fall in this love
to see how deep it truly is

Let's prove the myths to be
right or— wrong

Let's see if our vow of trust
is strong enough
to sink us to the seas
floors

II.   We finally jump in, and we begin to
grow farther away from the surface

We close our eyes
and share our air

III.   We float...
float back to the top
where the waves carry us back
to where we began

We are now thieves again
but we no longer
take from each other

Falling just wasn't meant for us

5 07.93

Geneva, Thursday
(This is a piece based off of a person named Geneva. I created her for a workshop, so this is written from Geneva's perspective)

1
Witty yet miniscule
a rascal covered in fur and skin
my companion for life
a woman's best friend

#2
Fire breathing pen
ink coated lips
armless, legless pen
yet— walking on paper
and grabbing my words
from my mind
to yours

Your ink coated mind
your ink coated heart
a woman's bleeding friend

#3
Lipless— eyeless
You can't speak to me
you can't see me

Breathless— touch—less
you don't breathe me
you don't feel me

#4
I hear your teeth jitter
when you're near me

I hear your eyelids flap
I hear your lungs minimize—
squeeze

I hear her moan, when you touch her
but I don't moan when you touch me
you don't need me
we're not lovers, we're not friends

5.01.93

I Know

I've never seen the sun kiss the moon
I've never heard echoes in the woods
created from lost falsettos— lost goodbyes
I've never felt the thump of a lion's heart

                    I don't know much

I've seen you
I've heard you
I've felt you
                    I know *love*…

5 07 93

June 30th

Why do I always try to find love
in the wrong women?

The ones who erupt with affection
but show subtle expression

The Nubian princess's soaking their
silks in the silver streams of the lagoons
the too late(s)
the too soon(s)

The June flings—
pageant winners
that I only see on occasions
resembling full moons—
Hailey's Comet

The porcelain skinned queen's
too fast
too rapid
so beautiful and solid
yet so transparent
and empty

The gold hearted lovers
trophy women—
shine for everyone

held by everyone
loved by everyone
but themselves

Forgotten by everyone
dropped by everyone
and themselves

The outstanding
that manage to remain *inside*
where they believe they belong

Changing to fit in a puzzle
of pieces
bending and creasing themselves
in order to find a matching piece—
shape shifters

The one's that enjoy
being chased
the long winded
the sprinters

The masked women of the night
the unmasked women of the morning
faceless but energetic when wearing the
mask
lifeless and careless when not wearing the
mask

making me want to say
"put on the mask
I don't know you"

Why can't I ever find love with
the right women
why can't I tell wrong from right

Why do all of the wrong women
try to find love in me,

Just because…

5 01.93

Dreaming Forever: Thoughts

Moon Light: September 18th 2009

In the middle of the night, I usually find myself
staring towards the heavens

I look at the stars and the moon
and they look back at me in light

The vibe they give off
is tangible

You can feel it
I look up and think about everything

I feel secure but unsure of
what the next day will bring

But I indulge in the practice of
living for the moment

And the night dresses itself
in beautiful starry skies
so how could I complain
when I am blessed with a view
comparable to new born love

Such a view
makes me think all the pain and
misfortune isn't worth thinking about

5.07.93

Charlie Love: September 20th 2009

I've walked a guided path
on the pavements
I've seen glimpses of good
and bad
I've absorbed for knowledge
and experience—
but I've done this alone

I needed to do it on my own
to develop my own character
to discover myself
to learn and to correct
to love and to live

"In the attitude of silence the soul finds the path in
a clearer light, and what is elusive and deceptive
resolves itself into crystal clearness. Our life is a
long and arduous quest after Truth." — Mahatma
Gandhi

5.01.93

165

The Key: October 3rd 2009

I just have to keep writing
it's all I can do.

"The key is hope" —Scott Mescudi

Passionate: November 23rd 2009

You live one life

I've been told that
to fulfill destiny brings one to a feeling of bliss—
of happiness in its eternal form

To have a bit of affection for something fairly
stimulates the mind but to have a love for
something (God) that is not tangible is divine

"Brother, to thy faith add knowledge." – St. Paul

Passionate II: January 6th 2010

Passion…
a word with no need
of justification through color or text,

A *belief* I hold
near to my heart—

Because when witnessed
upon sight
the feeling it gives you
is— *unbelievable*

Autumn Leaves: January 6th 2010

Autumn leaves discover
what others overlook

The beauty created through
change

So subtle— such a modest appeal
but it deserves to feel proud
it deserves color

But also understands that
all that becomes
beautiful—

Must begin as this

Must begin to love its beautiful existence
before others do

That is how one truly blossoms
the understanding
of how beauty resides on the inside

Art: February 8th 2010

Past events that create a collage of who
I once was
allow me to paint a picture of what
I am becoming

Brush stroke—
after brush stroke

As an artist
I guess that is why
when a process of dedication
is completed and an *unremarkable* product is
produced
it is called *state of the art*

5 01 93

The Coming: March 2nd 2010

I have a likeness for what may be beneath,
but a love for what is above

Still climbing

Gepetto: March 3rd 2010

Each breath you exhale is disowned and
you will never get them back... you can only honor
them by cherishing the next one

Gatsby: April 11th 2010

You can fantasize
about receiving your *it*
in reality
that *it* you memorize and
decorate with the pseudonym of perfection

But once you feel *it*
the texture—
but once you see *it*
the figure
and once *it* is
right there before you

You have to think about all
you have done to get to *it*—
and ask yourself

was *it* really worth *it*

Dolapo: May 1st 2010

My goal is not only to
display peace and love
through emotion
but also to illustrate the different
experiences that leave long lasting
impressions on my life
and those who I come in contact with

In hope of bringing joy and understanding
into fruition for all people

— Dolapo Demuren

"When the power of love overcomes the love of
power , the world will know peace." — Jimi
Hendrix

Subtle Sounds: May 16th 2010

Lights flicker—
like their life's
in a hurry
to reach end
synonymous to
an insoluble man
going through phases
influenced by
forlorn intentions

You have to understand
that I race
that trend
and try to erase
that trend

In hope that you will see
what your eye's
have a longing for

In hope that you will prevent
yourself from relying on hopelessness
as an inescapable justice

But
of all things
I just hope that you will

listen—

Hear me

5.07.93

Give it All of You: May 30th 2010

Honest efforts that end in
failures aren't necessarily defeats.
Your reactions to the
failures are what define the failures.

Unfortunate losses and disappointments
are experiences to learn from
and these experiences vary from person
to person, but the solution is universal.

I understand it hurts,
I may or may not know
of this pain you speak of
but I do know that wounds heal

You have to remember
perseverance breeds achievement

5 01 93

Greatness: May 30th 2010

When you know that you are the
best at what you do
and you let your humbleness
control your urges
to boast
by committing those moments
to ones of silence

You and those around you
witness one of the best feelings
in the world—

Greatness

5.07.93

Tony: June 5th 2010

I was talking to one of my closest friends, Tony, today and as the conversation went along he ended up saying "we're getting old." We are both seventeen, but he said this because we've known each other for years now and we've seen each other grow up at a pace that has allowed us to realize time is feeble. Throughout the past year or so he's been one of the only people that I could rely on and trust. We have been through a lot together and we have helped each other get over things such as excessive braggadocio and pain from disappointments. Overall we have grown up together and managed to grow closer through our hardships in the process.

We have a lot more to live Tony.
We'll be alright

5 07 93

The Lovers: June 15th 2010

We love because we believe in happiness' eternity.
We love because we believe love allows us to enter
another person's heaven

We love because, we live
and we live to love

All Night: July 2nd 2010

I thought I found her
But I'll never see her again

Yesterday
she was in my arms

Today I'm left with memories and
fascinations

I'll just have to live with the fact of knowing that
someday we'll both belong to other people

The Explanation: July 5th 2010

Inner motives and emotions are usually never
brought to surface, but once an artist chooses to
show what is inside
you have to be ready to receive it
because it may never happen again
the organic essence of the artist
may never be able to be attained or
embraced in the future
due to artistic evolution

You have to open your eyes
you have to breathe it as if it is needed

But if you don't want to see the truth behind the
artist's craft
because you are afraid of seeing the reality
of the person who inspires you

It's fine
you can miss it
all you have to do is
blink

But just know that
it may never happen again

Women: July 6th 2010

I just want to take this entry as an opportunity to express my immeasurable love for women. I love women with all of the love I have and I wish that every man proceeds to do the same. I understand that there is a holiday recognized for mothers and I am grateful for the creation of that day but I honestly believe that there should also be a day taken out of the year to recognize the beauty and strength of all women around the world. Women can be described in no other way than beautiful and I wish that all men will soon reach the realization that without our mothers, sisters and daughters we are nothing. We need to respect and love women because truly they are the pillars of our lives.

Mom
Grace
Amara Nwosu
Shira Singelenberg
Jasmine Whittington
Courtney Rowe
Kristina Austin
Maura Johnson
Courtney Skolnick
Salam Abdul Ali
Tinika Williams

To all the women who have ever cared for me or
taken care of me
throughout the course of my life

To all the women who have allowed me to be a
part of their lives

To all the women who have kept me level headed
through instilling steadfastness in me

I love you all

5 01 93

Drifting Far Off: August 4th 2010

I feel that I'm going through life
absorbing periods of contemplation, tribulation and
trial

To the point where I have begun to abandon
thoughts of the conditions of my growth
until I begin to worry about them
and realize all of the opportunities I've missed
because of all of the successes I've had

"It is a pity that, as one gradually gains experience,
one loses one's youth." – Vincent Van Gogh

The Romanticist's Entry: August 6th 2010

Often people forget who to comfort and who to
love

They become entranced by the unstable conditions
of work and temporary content

And within time they undergo stages of
dissatisfaction
and revelations of their mistakes

Because mirages of happiness never last
they turn into mares and
appear distilled in mirrors
always looking clearer in the past

No one should allow their profession
to limit the comfort they give to the person they
love

Because if they do
they may gain something
but they may also lose everything
and ultimately trade love for nothing

5 07 93

Individuality: August 20th 2010

I feel that in certain areas of reality, individuality is looked down upon and discouraged.

People must learn to love themselves and appreciate individuality, as well as loving others for who they are

Because no one can be neither you nor me and that is the beauty of individuality

My Mother: August 23rd 2010

"Often one develops an admiration for strength through comic book super heroes, famous leaders or courageous war heroes. But I find my admiration for strength somewhere else.

I find it in my mother, the strongest woman in the world. Through her I have learned to admire the greatest strength of all.

The strength of love"

—Dolapo Demuren

Differences start with each of us. I believe we can each make a difference through fostering good will using love for the purposes of serenity and peace. We can all make our world a better place if we use our freedom to serve one another with love.

—Dolapo Demuren

Peace & Love

I love you Grace

About the Author

All Photography by Shira Singelenberg

Dolapo Demuren is a 17 year old High School student. He is an avid reader, a fan of all aspects of art and also enjoys many genres of music.

Give the gift of

DREAMING FOREVER: LIFEMARE EDITION

To your friends and associates

☐ Yes I want _____ copies of Dreaming Forever Lifemare Edition at $9.95 each plus $4.95 shipping per book (Maryland residents please add 6% sales tax per book). Canadian orders must be accompanied by a postal money order in U.S. Funds. Please allow 15 days for delivery.

☐ Yes I am interested in having Dolapo Demuren speak or read his poetry to our organization, school, association or company. Please send information.

My check or money order payable to A Better Tomorrow Publishing for $_____ is enclosed

Please charge my: ☐ Visa ☐ MasterCard ☐ Discover ☐ American Express

Name_____

Organization_____

Address _____

City/State/Zip_____

Phone _____

Email_____

Card Number _____

Exp. Date _____

Signature _____

A Better Tomorrow Publishing
P.O. Box 2975
Upper Marlboro, MD 20773—2975
Call your credit card order to: 1—866—980—8541
Fax: 240—667—7252 www.abtpub.com